DR. GEO

MW01225478

LIFE IN EXTREME ENVIRONMENTS™

LIFE IN THE ARCTIC

SHELDON BROOKS

rosen
central™

The Rosen Publishing Group, Inc., New York

To Arembepe and the folks at Oca Ecatú

Published in 2004 by The Rosen Publishing Group, Inc.
29 East 21st Street, New York, NY 10010

₃₀₀₀

Copyright © 2004 by The Rosen Publishing Group, Inc.

First Edition

Library of Congress Cataloging-in-Publication Data

Brooks, Sheldon, 1958–
Life in the Arctic/Sheldon Brooks.— 1st ed.
    p. cm.—(Life in extreme environments)
Summary: Defines the Arctic and indicates how plants, animals, and humans learn to survive in this extreme environment. Includes bibliographical references and index.
ISBN 0-8239-3984-7 (lib. bdg.)
1. Natural history—Arctic regions—Juvenile literature. 2. Cold adaptation—Arctic regions—Juvenile literature. 3. Arctic peoples—Juvenile literature. [1. Natural history—Arctic regions. 2. Cold adaptation. 3. Arctic peoples. 4. Arctic regions.]
I. Title. II. Series.
QH84.1.B76 2003
508.311'3—dc21

2003000721

Manufactured in the United States of America

DR. GEORGE M. WEIR

CONTENTS

INTRODUCTION: THE EXTREME NORTH

The Arctic region that circles the top of the world and surrounds the North Pole is one of the coldest, iciest, and most isolated areas on the planet. What we call the Arctic is generally, though not exclusively, the area that lies north of the Arctic Circle—an imaginary line that rings the North Pole at a latitude of approximately 66.5 degrees north. At the Arctic Circle, the sun never sets on the longest day of the year (usually June 21). It also never rises on the shortest day of the year (usually December 21).

It is about 1,680 miles (2,700 kilometers) from the Arctic Circle to the North Pole. Walking north from the Arctic Circle, the farther you go, the more hours of nonstop daylight you get in the summer and nonstop night in the winter. For example, in Grise Fiord, a Canadian community 650 miles (1,050 km) north of the Arctic Circle, the sun doesn't set for seventy-seven days during the summer. However, if endless sunshine sounds like fun, remember there is a downside: In the middle of winter, Grise Fiord's residents have to put up with seventy-seven days of endless night.

When you finally reach the North Pole, the situation is even more radical. Six months of continuous daylight are followed by a half-year of darkness.

When we think of the Arctic, we tend to think of North America (Canada and Alaska). But the Arctic also spans the northern portions of Europe (Scandinavia), Asia (Russia), and Greenland, the planet's largest island. It has an ocean of its own—the Arctic Ocean—which is the smallest of the world's oceans. It is also the most frozen of all the oceans. Even in the middle of the summer, 75 percent of the ocean remains covered in ice.

You may be wondering how anything or anybody could possibly live in the midst of so much ice and snow. How can plants, animals, and people survive eight to nine months of winter in which the highest temperature is 20° Fahrenheit (-7° Celsius) and the lowest temperature is -70°F (-57°C)? And this is excluding the windchill factor produced by howling Arctic winds, which sends the temperature plummeting even lower.

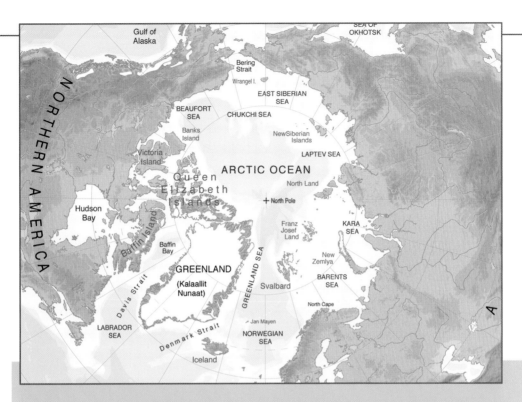

The Arctic Ocean is the smallest of the world's five oceans, although it stretches nearly 9 million square miles (about 14 million square km) and includes Baffin Bay, the Barents Sea, the Beaufort Sea, the Chukchi Sea, the East Siberian Sea, the Greenland Sea, Hudson Bay, the Hudson Strait, the Kara Sea, the Laptev Sea, and the Northwest Passage.

Surprisingly, there are plants, animals, and people who inhabit the Arctic. In order to survive, plants and animals have unique and often quite fantastic characteristics and capabilities. Take the Arctic fox, which differs in several ways from other foxes. While its paws are padded with thick fur, its gleaming white coat captures and keeps heat better than that of any other land mammal on the earth. In one study, an Arctic fox was exposed to -112°F (-80°C) temperatures for an hour and didn't so much as shiver.

The Arctic fox is supremely adapted to live in the cold climate of the Arctic deserts. They only weigh from 6 to 10 pounds (2.72 to 4.5 kilograms) when full-grown, about the size of a domestic cat. They are omnivorous, but mainly hunt the Arctic lemming for food.

Meanwhile, humans who long ago migrated to the Arctic adapted to the climate and geography, creating a culture and way of life that allowed them to live in harmony with such extreme conditions. Imagine camping out in a house made of blocks of snow with windows constructed from see-through seal intestines. Or think of eating "Eskimo ice cream," made from a frothy mixture of seal oil, chewed caribou fat, and amber-colored cloudberries.

However, conditions in the Arctic aren't always so extreme. Come summer, the temperature rises, sometimes up to 80°F (27°C). The sun's golden rays light up fields of multi-colored wildflowers that resemble beautiful tapestries. When the snow melts, strange and wonderful landscapes become visible. Slow-flowing rivers of ice—called glaciers—leave behind striped patterns of dirt and pebbles in fantastic designs. Also impressive are pingos—cone-shaped hills with cores of pure ice that rise out of the ground, sometimes as high as 150 feet (46 meters).

Whether hot or cold, light or night, the Arctic is nonetheless one of the planet's most fascinating regions. In the following chapters, you'll learn about some of its most interesting inhabitants and how they survive in such an extreme environment.

CHAPTER ONE

TUNDRA: WHERE THE TREES STOP

When traveling north, there is one way to tell when you've hit the Arctic—quite simply, you run out of trees. Subarctic regions are covered by taiga, a Russian word that refers to a moist forest of conifers. A more popular nickname for taiga is "spruce-moose" because the region is home to many moose, tends to have many hardy spruce trees, and has a mossy forest floor. If you walk north through the taiga, the thick forests of black and white spruce and pine gradually thin out while the trees themselves become shorter. Sometimes, these dwarf trees stand no taller than 3 feet (0.91 m).

Even the dwarf trees disappear altogether at the timberline—an imaginary line circling the northern regions of the globe where the average temperature in the warmest months of summer is 50°F (10°C). Any colder than this and even the toughest of trees can't survive.

What comes after taiga is tundra. Tundra is a Russian word that means a marshy area without trees. Arctic tundra is a biome of its own. A biome, or ecosystem, is a geographic region that has its own specific types of plants and animals living within it. Although tundra covers 20 percent of the earth's surface, it possesses only a few species of plants. There are several reasons for this. One is the absence of sunlight, which plants need to give them energy to grow. Second, the biome's cold temperatures can freeze and kill plants. A further problem is the Arctic soil, which is covered with snow for nine to ten months of the

MAMMOTH DISCOVERY

Permafrost is like a giant freezer where entire plants and animals—hair, skin, warts, and all—can be perfectly preserved for thousands of years. In 1951, scientists in Alaska uncovered a 30,000-year-old "super-bison."

Meanwhile, in Russia, people frequently come across the frozen bodies of gigantic woolly mammoths. To date, more than 120,000 of these big, hairy Arctic elephants have been dug out of the earth.

year. Not only does this soil lack nutrients, but it is also very shallow. This is because a layer of frozen ground called permafrost lies a few feet beneath the earth's surface.

While the surface of the earth freezes in winter and thaws out in summer, the permafrost below it, as its name implies, stays permanently frozen. In some places, permafrost is 2,000 feet (600 m) deep. Permafrost is one major reason trees or tall plants with deep roots can't grow in the tundra. Instead, tundra plants are small, with shallow roots.

A DESERT WITH SOGGY SOIL

In an average year, the tundra receives between 12 to 20 inches (31 to 51 centimeters) of snow. Melted down and added to the annual rainfall, this is about the same amount of precipitation that might fall in the Sahara Desert. How, then, do you explain the fact that the tundra is covered with mountainous snowbanks in the winter and bogs, marshes, and lakes in the summer?

So much snow is explained by low temperatures and reduced amounts of sunlight. Because of these two conditions, even in the summer, very little snow actually melts. Moreover, the fierce Arctic winds blow the snow into tall drifts, where it piles up month after month and even year after year.

Snow that does melt in the summer seeps into the earth, but only as far as the permafrost. Unable to be absorbed by the

These houses in Kangaamiut, Greenland, are built up on stilts to avoid melting the permafrost. Hot water pipes and boilers also have to be built above ground and insulated from the permafrost to preserve them.

frozen ground, it collects in the soil, forming ponds and marshes. The fact that the Arctic sun is weak and temperatures remain cool, even in the summer, means that this water is evaporated into the air at a very slow rate.

Both soggy soil and permafrost make it tricky for people to actually live on the tundra. Heat generated by a home warms the ground, causing even the permafrost to melt and become mushy. In order not to wind up in a sinking house, many Arctic residents build their homes on stilts, creating a space between the house and the permafrost.

A (VERY SHORT) YEAR IN THE LIFE OF AN ARCTIC PLANT

For most of the year, tundra plants remain dormant, or sleeping, under a blanket of snow. The snow actually protects them from strong cold winds. Only in May, when the first rays of sunlight begin to melt the snow, do the first plant shoots appear.

Once June arrives and the air gets warmer, plants on the tundra really begin to grow. Even though the sun's rays are weak in the summer, the fact that it almost never sets means that the tundra receives as much solar energy as the Tropics. Nevertheless, plants only have until August—a short ten to fourteen weeks—to grow, flower, and set seed.

The flowering period is a particularly beautiful time to be on the tundra. For example, during late summer in the southern Arctic, you can see up to 100 different kinds of wildflowers in bloom. And the colors are quite fantastic: from crimson lousewort and purple oxytropes to yellow Arctic poppies and brilliant bluebells.

By September, the growth cycle is already over, and plants must prepare again for winter. Water and pigments seep out of the bright green leaves and stems to be stored

The dwarf willow plant *(Salix arctica)* is a member of the willow tree family. A small shrub that can only grow as high as 8 inches (20.32 cm), it thrives in tundra and alpine regions. Caribou often eat the leaves in summer and the bark during winter when other food is scarce.

underground in the roots of the plants. This process results in the tundra's brilliant fall colors that rival those of the forests of northeastern Canada and the United States. Dwarf birches and heathers turn shades of orange, red, and amber while bright blueberries and cranberries can be found everywhere.

PLANT SURVIVAL STRATEGIES

For plants, growing up on the tundra is no easy task. After all, there is very little warmth and light. Nevertheless, tundra plants have adopted various survival strategies that allow them to live in the middle of the Arctic.

Grow Low

Plants on the tundra grow close to the ground. Although poor soil limits height, another reason for keeping a low profile is that the air is warmer near the ground. This is because the soil is dark and thus absorbs heat.

Short, Dark, and Hairy

In order to warm up quickly and retain heat, many Arctic plants are dark in color and are fuzzy or hairy. Hair traps warmth and, like a coat, protects the plant from the cold. Also, less heat is lost when plants come in small and compact forms like cushions, and grow together in protective clumps.

Evergreen

Instead of losing their leaves in the autumn, some tundra plants keep them throughout the winter. These evergreens get a head start on the next growing season.

Outhouse Effect

Tall plants such as monkshood and larkspur thrive by growing in areas where snowy owls perch, eat, and do their business.

Owl droppings are great fertilizers. Plants also thrive in areas that lemmings and foxes use as "outhouses."

A BERRY GOOD SOURCE OF FOOD

There are lots of berries on the tundra, and just about every Arctic resident, from birds and bears to hares and humans, depends upon these fruits. One type of Arctic berry is such a big part of the grizzly bear's diet that it is known as the bearberry. Another grizzly favorite is the tiny red soap-berry—bears can eat two hundred thousand of these in just one day!

In autumn, melting sea ice forces polar bears ashore, where these big white bears trade their usual diet of seals for shiny black crowberries. Around this time, it is common to run into polar bears with bright purple berry stains around their mouths. Unlike most berries, crowberries stay on the plant throughout the winter, and they are eaten frozen by migrating geese who fly north early before there is much other food available. They are also gathered by humans who eat them mixed with blubber.

This grizzly bear is eating soapberries in Denali National Park, Alaska. Besides berries, grizzly bears will eat carrion, smaller animals, fish, and animals weakened by disease or age. They are often attracted to food that is carried or left behind by humans, which is why they sometimes pose a threat to hikers and campers.

LICHENS

In the most northern regions of the Arctic, not even plants can survive. Basically, the only vegetation found in this area—which is classified as polar desert—is lichen. Lichen isn't a plant but a plantlike type of vegetation that is a mixture of fungus and algae. There are more than twenty thousand different kinds of lichens in the world. Around one thousand are native to the Arctic.

It is no wonder that lichens are the toughest and oldest plants on the earth. There is no place in the world that is too cold, too hot, or too dry for them. This explains why they are found in the coldest spots of the Arctic, where they cling to rocks, bark, bones, caribou antlers, and even animal dung. Because they don't have roots, lichens can grow anywhere. All they need to survive is moisture from the air.

Lichens have been known to survive temperatures as cold as -460°F (-273°C). This explains why some have been around for thousands of years, dating back to the earliest days of human life.

When lichen is wet, walking on it is like stepping on a slippery rubber mat. However, when dry, it can be so delicate that it crunches and flakes off beneath your feet. Multicolored lichens—from gray and white to brilliant greens, reds, and oranges—brighten up otherwise bleak northern landscapes.

Particularly beautiful is jewel lichen. A rich orange color, it is known by the Inuit of northern Greenland as *sunain anak*, meaning "the sun's excrement."

Rich in nutrients, lichens are sometimes the best and only food option available for Arctic residents. During the winter, caribou survive by feasting on lichen known as reindeer moss. Humans also eat lichen, although they must boil out some of its strong acids beforehand. Many early explorers of the Canadian Arctic ate lichen as a last resort to prevent starvation. Unfortunately, in their desperation, they often tore it off the rocks and swallowed it raw, which gave them upset stomachs and diarrhea.

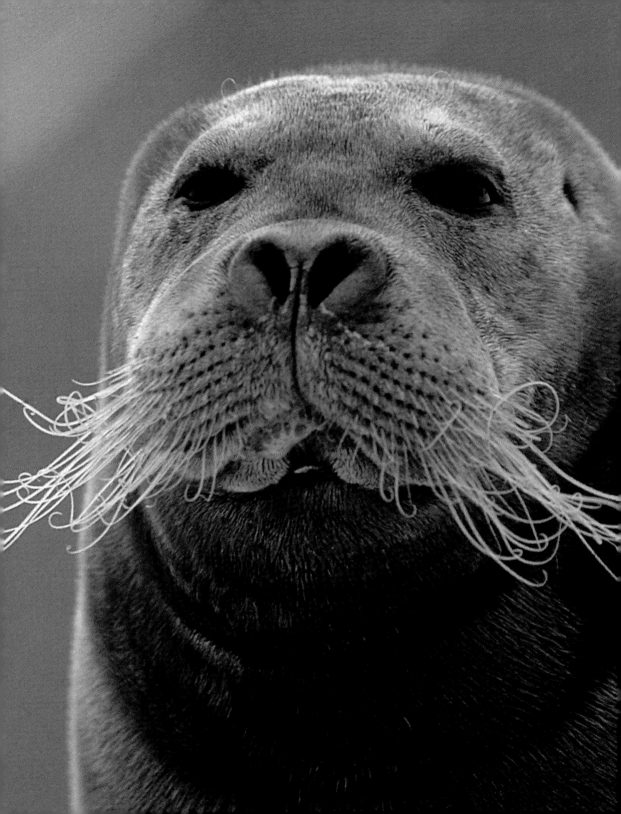

CHAPTER TWO

WHERE THE SUN NEVER SETS

Because they live in such a remote, seldom-visited region where conditions have forced them to adapt in surprising ways, many Arctic animals seem very exotic to us. After all, it's not every day you run into the following:

- A 6-foot-long (2-meter-long), 750-pound (340-kg) bearded seal whose incredibly sensitive whiskers contain nerve fibers to help it find its way to breathing holes when swimming beneath ice.

A bearded seal is the largest seal found in the Alaskan seas. They mainly eat crab, shrimp, clams, and snails, and are hunted for their skin, blubber, and meat.

- Spectacled eider ducks who appear to be wearing glasses and whose soft feathers are used to stuff warm eiderdown sleeping bags, quilts, and ski jackets.

- Packs of white-coated Arctic wolves—the only wolves on the planet who catch and eat fish.

- Small (and noisy) Arctic rodents called singing voles who spend all summer collecting roots, leaves, and other greens,

Spectacled eider ducks are one of four kinds of seafaring ducks that breed in Alaska. Since they spend most of their lives far out at sea, they have not been well studied. However, since the early 1970s, the number of spectacled eiders in western Alaska has declined by more than 90 percent. In 1993, the spectacled eider was designated a threatened species under the U.S. Endangered Species Act.

only to have their goods stolen and eaten by grizzly bears or humans in search of vegetables.

- Flying Arctic seabirds called auks. During mating season, their beaks turn brilliant shades of orange and yellow in order to attract mates.

- The 2,650-pound (1,200-kg) narwhal with a single 8-foot-long (2.5-meter-long) tusk (actually a giant tooth), which for centuries was thought to be the magic horn of a unicorn.

TEMPORARY RESIDENTS

As is the case with plants, the Arctic is home to fewer animal species than other warmer biomes on the earth. Ultimately, very few animals can actually put up with living in the Arctic. And many of those who live north of the Arctic Circle do so on a part-time basis. They take advantage of the long summer days before migrating south in the autumn when the cold and darkness begin to set in. Millions of ducks, geese, gulls, loons, and sandpipers are temporary tundra residents, flying north each year in search of great nesting spots and the sudden banquet of edible plants and insects. One visitor in particular, a bird called the Arctic tern, enjoys the best of two worlds.

Each year, the tern spends summers in the Arctic. When autumn comes to the Northern Hemisphere, the tern sets out on

The Arctic tern's remarkable journey from the Arctic to the Antarctic and back is equivalent to flying the entire circumference of the earth. They live on average about thirty years, and can travel over 650,000 miles (about one million km) in their lifetimes.

a cross-continental journey to the Antarctic, arriving just in time to take advantage of a second summer in the Southern Hemisphere. Of course, the tern pays a price for its back-to-back summers. It spends most of its twenty-five-year life span in transit. The 22,000-mile (36,000-km) round-trip journey is the longest recorded migration of any creature on the earth.

Another famous Arctic migrant is the caribou. In herds that number hundreds of thousands, these antlered animals travel from the tundra to the taiga and back again—a journey that can total 2,700 miles (4,400 km). The sight of a migrating herd is quite spectacular.

Like moose, male caribou have spectacular antlers, which begin to grow every spring. By autumn, which is mating season, they are fully grown, measuring up to 4 feet (1.4 m) in length—and ready for action. For males, antlers are a way of advertising to females what great mates they'd make. The older and healthier the caribou, the bigger the antlers. And each year, the antlers increase in size.

Antlers come in handy when males start butting heads—literally—over potential female mates.

Once breeding is over, males lose their antlers until the following year. This explains the estimated two million sets of caribou antlers that clutter up the Canadian tundra each year. However, with so many lost horns, how come nobody's constantly tripping over antlers in the Arctic? Because the antlers

The antlers shed by a caribou provide food and minerals to tundra foragers and even other caribou. Humans also utilize antlers to make tools like needles, spoons, and combs, as well as elaborate carvings.

are such an excellent source of calcium and other important minerals, health-conscious lemmings, voles, ground squirrels, and even caribou themselves chomp on discarded antlers regularly. This explains how the tundra is kept tidy.

SEA MAMMALS

The Arctic Ocean and the Arctic ice that floats upon it are home to some of the world's largest and most interesting animals.

Seals

Six different types of seals live in the Arctic: ringed, spotted, bearded, ribbon, harp, and hooded. In early spring, seal mothers give birth to a single pup on the sea ice. However, the ice can easily break into pieces, separating mother and pup. Also, it can crumble and dump the newborn seal into the freezing water. Because of these risks, baby seals need to quickly grow protective blubber—layers of warm fat.

It is for this reason that the hooded seal has the shortest nursing period of any mammal on the earth. Hooded seal pups feed on their mother's milk for only four days. During that time, a pup balloons from 48 pounds (22 kg) to 92 pounds (42 kg)! This is the equivalent of one person wolfing down sixty-two hamburgers, twenty-five orders of fries, twelve chocolate milk shakes, and fifteen fudge sundaes in one day.

A hooded seal pup nurses on the sea ice in Newfoundland. After four days of nursing, the pup will nearly double in size, and will then be weaned and left to fend for itself. They are named "hooded" because the adult males have a bizarre inflatable "hood" of skin on their heads that puffs up when they are competing for mates.

Such rapid weight gain is due to the fact that a mother seal's milk is more than twice as thick as whipped cream. While regular cows' milk has 4 percent fat and whipped cream has 30 percent fat, a mother seal's milk contains between 50 and 70 percent fat.

Walruses

The massive, wrinkled, roly-poly walrus is a strange-looking animal that would be totally lost if it weren't for its two enormous

Male and female walruses congregate in separate herds that can sometimes include thousands of animals. In 1950, the walrus seemed to be headed for extinction, and walrus hunting was widely banned. The walrus is now protected, and in the United States, only indigenous people in Alaska are permitted to hunt them for food.

front teeth. These two ivory tusks, which can grow to 30 inches (75 cm) in length, are extremely useful. They are used for chopping holes in sea ice, as weapons against enemy hunters such as polar bears and killer whales, and to help support the walrus when he or she needs to climb up onto the ice for some rest and relaxation.

When it's time to eat, walruses comb the ocean floors for seafood such as clams, mussels, and crabs. They can put away 190 pounds (85 kg) of seafood in one day. Their thick tongues and strong cheek muscles produce a suction pump that allows them to suck clams or mussels right out of the shell and into their mouths.

Whales

Only three of the planet's seventy-six types of whales are equipped to deal with icy Arctic seas. Bowhead and beluga whales are both experts at navigating ice-covered waters and can travel for twenty minutes beneath the ice without coming up for air. If no airholes are in sight, both whales butt through the thick ice (sometimes up to 25 inches [60 cm] thick) with their heads in order to catch their breath. Even though they have protective padding around their blow-holes, many whales often have scars from smacking their heads against the ice.

The third type of Arctic whale is the narwhal with its famous unicorn-like horn. For centuries, people wondered about the use of this overgrown tooth. It was discovered that male narwhals, like caribou, use the tusk as a showpiece to impress potential mates. Rival narwhal suitors even use their tusks like swords to fence with one another. For this reason, many have broken tusks as well as scars on their heads.

CHAPTER THREE

WHEN THE GOING GETS COLD

Few animals stick around the Arctic once the summer crowd has moved south. Those who do remain are naturally equipped to deal with the dark, cold days of a long Arctic winter.

PERMANENT RESIDENTS

Musk oxen have been living in the tundra for thousands of years. Although they look like big, shaggy bison, they are actually related to the sheep family. Musk oxen survive the winters because of their long, warm fur, a strand of which can measure 3 feet (0.91 m). In fact, these super-coats come equipped

Musk oxen on Nunivak Island, Alaska. Their only natural enemies are wolves and polar bears. They are called "musk oxen" because during their breeding season, they put out a musky scent from their facial glands.

with two layers: the outside boasts long, dark protective hair, while beneath is a layer of soft, warm fur. During the summer, musk oxen shed this undercoat. Prized for its silkiness, the fur is gathered by the Inuit and knit into warm clothing.

Another large mammal that has no problem surviving the winter is the wolverine. Its nasty reputation as a scavenger has led to many nicknames, including "hyena of the north," "glutton," and "devil bear." Resembling a small bear, the wolverine is actually the largest land member of the weasel family. They eat everything from berries, birds' eggs, and leftover animal carcasses to nutrient-rich caribou bones.

Cunning and fearless, wolverines often steal other animals' leftovers and hide them in holes to be dug up in the winter. Wolverines deal well with winter weather because their fur never becomes matted or encrusted with ice from breath condensation. Because of this, the Inuit use wolverine fur to line the hoods of their parkas.

Polar bears also have highly protective fur coats, but theirs are creamy white. Polar bears and their cousins— brown, or grizzly, bears—are the two largest bear species in the world and the only ones to inhabit the Arctic. Both bears can grow to a height of 8 feet (2.4 m) and weigh up to 1,600 pounds (726 kg).

Although polar bears are meat eaters and grizzlies are omnivores, the lack of food during the winter has made

Polar bears are one of the largest land carnivores. Their heavy coats can make them overheat even in the Arctic, so they tend to move slowly and nap frequently to conserve energy. They hunt seals and walruses by waiting near holes in the ice (like the one above), where their prey might come up to breathe. They can also smell and track prey over a great distance—which can make them a danger to unwary humans.

both flexible eaters. Polar bears sometimes feast on berries, roots, and birds' eggs, while grizzlies resort to eating fish, caribou, and even musk oxen.

With their waterproof coats, polar bears can easily dive into the freezing Arctic Ocean or move around on ice. They can navigate the ice with ease because of their coarse, sandpaper-like foot pads, which prevent them from slipping. Researchers from the Ford Motor Company were so impressed by these natural soles that they copied the design for slip-resistant footwear for their workers.

Meanwhile, land-bound grizzlies spend their winters curled up in hibernation. Bears lie dormant (often for up to six months) in order to conserve heat and energy. During this period, their heart rates drop from forty to seventy beats per minute to eight to twelve beats, and they don't eat, drink, or go to the bathroom. If a human were to try such a stunt, he or she would die in less than a week.

PERMANENT RESIDENTS' SURVIVAL STRATEGIES

Surprisingly, few of the animals that spend all year in the Arctic actually do hibernate. Instead, they resort to a variety of other survival strategies to make it through the winter.

RABBIT TRICKS

The white-coated Arctic hare, which is three times as heavy as its cousins to the south, hops around on its hind legs like a kangaroo. Traveling in herds of up to twenty-five thousand, these hares are quite a sight when in motion. When food is scarce, these resourceful rabbits eat their own droppings.

Although it is prey for foxes, owls, wolves, and bears, the Arctic hare is a tough survivor. It will eat mosses, lichens, buds, berries, seaweed, bark, willow twigs and roots, and even the meat from hunters' traps.

Although polar bears (except for pregnant females) do not hibernate, most other bear species do. Grizzly bears like this one may stay in their dens up to six months in the coldest climates. They survive by lowering their heart rate and body temperature and slowing their breathing to conserve energy.

- Antifreeze. Having body fluids freeze up is a big danger to small Arctic animals. To fight freezing, some creatures dehydrate in the winter. They purposefully reduce their intake of liquids such as water so they will have less body fluid to freeze.

- Small parts. In general, Arctic animals have smaller arms, legs, ears, and snouts than similar species in warmer regions. For example, the ears of an Arctic fox are much smaller than those of a desert fox. Since they are more exposed to cold air, big ears or long tails freeze more

In the Arctic, timber wolves adapt by changing their coat color to white during the winter. They hunt lemmings, Arctic hares, musk oxen, and caribou, and eat every part of what they kill, including skin, fur, and bones.

easily. They also waste more of an animal's precious energy since it takes more effort to pump warm blood into a large body part.

- Change of color. In the summertime, many Arctic creatures have fur or feathers colored earthy brown or gray. However, in the fall, their coats gradually change to snowy white.

Such camouflage is both good and bad: while it helps potential prey (such as Arctic hares) stay hidden year-round, it also makes it easier for potential predators with changing coats such as Arctic foxes, snowy owls, and short-tailed weasels to sneak up on them.

Borealis Bonus

Those humans who are tough enough to stick out the winter months receive the bonus of witnessing the aurora borealis, or northern lights. The blue, green, and red lights that swirl

A spectacular springtime display of the aurora borealis in Alaska. Auroras can cause interference with power systems, transmission lines, industrial pipelines, radar systems, radio communications, and airplane navigational systems.

around the Arctic sky were believed by ancient Inuit to be the torches of spirits guiding souls to the land of happiness. In fact, auroras are caused by giant explosions of charged sun particles that come hurtling toward Earth's magnetic poles. Some Japanese couples even believe it is good luck to conceive their first child beneath an aurora display.

CHAPTER FOUR

PEOPLES OF THE ARCTIC

During an ice age hundreds of thousands of years ago, a land bridge connected the Arctic tip of Asia (Siberia) to the Arctic tip of North America (Alaska). Today, the bridge makes up the floor of the Bering Sea, a 56-mile (90-km) strip of ocean that separates the two continents. Between twenty thousand and thirty thousand years ago, the first of North America's native peoples crossed the bridge from Asia into what is today Canada and the United States.

When the ice age ended, many migrated north to the Arctic. Later, between 3000 and 1000 BC, they

Inuit whaling captains play cards in their tent before setting out on a bowhead whale hunting expedition. Of all the wildlife available to Inuit, the bowhead whale was certainly one of the most sought after. The fact that bowhead whales are slow swimmers and float (rather than sink) when killed made these animals a very important food source.

were joined by new Asian immigrants who had sailed across the Bering Sea in boats made of animal skins. Outsiders called these Arctic peoples "Eskimos." An Algonquian Indian word that means "eaters of raw meat," the term was used negatively to describe a supposedly savage people. To this day, North America's Arctic peoples prefer to refer to themselves as Inuit, which in their language, Inuktitut, means "the people."

Today, many native groups that share the same ancestry as the Inuit—the Aleuts, the Chukchi, and the Ami, for example—live throughout the world's Arctic regions. Their cultural habits and languages differ somewhat. However, their lifestyles and the traditional ways with which, for centuries, they have handled surviving in an extreme climate are quite similar.

Seventy Words for Snow

Language says a lot about a culture. That the Inuit have some seventy words for snow proves how deeply their lives revolve around the white Arctic powder. Here are just a few examples:

Apu–snow on the ground.

Aquilluaqqaqa–snow that is firm but not quite firm enough for an igloo.

Dethlok–snow deep enough to need snowshoes.

Ganik–falling snow.

Igluksaq–snow used for making an igloo.

Masak–wet snow typical of spring.

Piqtua–snow being blown around in a blizzard.

Pukak–powdery snow.

Qali–snow that collects on trees.

Siqoq–drifting snow.

LIVING OFF THE LAND

Traditionally, Arctic peoples have relied on hunting large mammals for their survival. For example, many Inuit living in

Caribou are a mainstay of the Arctic people's diet. Caribou migrate more than 1,000 miles (1,609 km) a year, farther than any other land mammal. They return to their birth place to give birth to their own young.

the Arctic interior planned their lives around the migration of caribou, following the enormous herds as they moved between tundra and taiga.

Caribou were extremely important to the Inuit. They were generally hunted with bows and arrows but sometimes with spears. A caribou's meat was one of the Inuit's main sources of food (the tongue and the nose were considered great delicacies). Most of the time, it was eaten raw. Cooking meat was difficult because firewood was so scarce. On the positive side, raw meat contains a high dosage of vitamin C (not found in cooked meat) that prevented the Inuit from getting diseases such as scurvy. Leftover meat could be dried in the sun or frozen in the permafrost to be eaten later.

Caribou hide was made into bedding, tents, canoes, and all sorts of equipment, ranging from dog harnesses and rope to fishnets and the webbing for snowshoes. Meanwhile, bones and antlers were used to make weapons, fishhooks, sewing needles, and the runners for dogsleds. And sinew (the stringy substance of the caribou's tendon) was used as string for bows and thread for sewing. Hides were also used for clothing. Women prepared them first by scraping off the fat and then chewing the skins to make them soft.

EDIBLE OPTIONS

If there was a shortage of caribou, the Inuit sometimes hunted musk oxen. Their shaggy coats made wonderfully warm clothing and bedding. Bears, however, were usually avoided. Not only are they extremely dangerous, but the polar bear's liver is poisonous to eat. And although bearskins made great bedding, they were too heavy for clothing. Furthermore, according to some native religious beliefs, bears and humans are distantly related.

In the spring, women and children often climbed up dangerous cliffs in search of birds' eggs. In the summer and early autumn, there were roots, herbs, and berries to be gathered. Everybody was usually thankful to have a change in the menu. When times were really tough, there

BLUBBER

Blubber is a layer of fat that covers the body of an animal like a big thick blanket. It keeps the animal from losing body heat. Many Arctic animals put on weight for the winter, but sea mammals such as seals, walruses, and whales have loads of blubber to keep them warm. In fact, the Arctic's biggest whale, the bowhead, can have a layer of blubber that is 20 inches (50 cm) thick.

To keep warm in the winter and build up energy reserves that make it possible not to eat for days at a time, many Arctic peoples eat whale blubber. Known as *muktuk*, this favorite food is eaten raw when fresh or boiled when it has been stored. Gram for gram, it contains more vitamin C than a lemon.

A man in Barrow, Alaska, eats muktuk as a snack.

An Inuit prepares to harpoon a bowhead whale in the Bering Sea. While most large-scale whale hunting is banned, indigenous peoples who depend on whale meat are still allowed to hunt them.

was always lichen and bark. Although not terribly mouth-watering, both could be boiled and made into soup.

LIVING OFF THE SEA

In much the same way, the livelihood of those people (such as the Aleuts) who lived on the Arctic coast and islands depended on the hunting of sea mammals. As with land mammals, every single part of the walruses, whales, and seals caught was used. Because there are no trees or even wood on the tundra, whalebones were used to make the frames of houses. Walrus hides were used to make walls and roofs, and their see-through guts were perfect for windows. Walrus intestines were also ideal for waterproof clothing such as parkas, mittens, and boots that kept hunters dry when they were at sea. Seal oil was used not only to cook food but also to heat homes and provide light.

Traditionally, there were two ways to hunt a seal: Since seals needed to come up from the sea for air every fifteen minutes or so, hunters would wait patiently near their breathing holes, armed with spears. The other way was in a boat, using a harpoon. Both methods were extremely dangerous. Hunters on ice risked slipping or breaking through into the ocean. Those on the sea risked having their boats overturned by fierce winds or by the hunted animals themselves. Drowning was frequent. Few Arctic people knew how to swim. Even if they did, the freezing water meant almost instant death from hypothermia.

Although most meals were meat based, Arctic peoples would sometimes add fish to their diet. Inuit women, children, and elders would often sit at ice holes with bark or leather fishing lines, waiting patiently for a bite. Meanwhile, in the freezing cold water, teams of men struggled to pull in heavy nets laden with fish.

Ice Inventions

Two ingenious inventions made life on the ice a little easier, not to mention safer.

- To prevent slipping on the ice, hunters invented ivory studs made from walrus tusks that were attached to the bottoms of their shoes. Like soccer cleats, they provided traction.

- To avoid eye damage from the blinding glare of sunlit ice, the Inuit were the first to invent snow goggles. Made out of wood with tiny slits for eyes, they were often carved in the likeness of seals.

GETTING AROUND

Getting around in the Arctic, particularly during the winter, was no easy matter. The changing climate and constantly migrating food supply meant that people were often on the move. Nevertheless, the Inuit and other peoples came up with some resourceful solutions.

By Land

Before the days of snowmobiles, cars, and trucks, Arctic people depended on sleds to get around, transport their belongings, and haul home edible wildlife they had hunted.

Originally, sleds—which could measure up to 30 feet (9 m) in length—were pulled by teams of half-tamed wolves. Over time, these wolves were bred with dogs and became known as huskies. Extremely important to Inuit survival, huskies were treated with great care. In fact, much time was spent hunting in order to feed the dogs their ration of seal and whale meat. After they died, the fur of much-loved huskies was often used to line the hood of a hunter's parka. However, as much as the dogs were valued, if faced with starvation, Inuit were sometimes forced to eat dogs.

When getting around on foot, Arctic people relied upon snowshoes that allowed them to walk on the surface of the snow. The snowshoes were adapted to various kinds of snow. Shorter ones were used for walking on packed snow, while six-footers (about 2 m) were more efficient on fresh snow. Hunting snowshoes helped hunters move over the snow more quickly than the caribou or moose they were chasing. The animals were slower because their hooves sank into snow—as opposed to quickly gliding over it.

A new territory called Nunavut was formed in Canada in 1999 to give Inuits more control over their government and their future. At left, Nunavut's new premier-elect, Paul Okauk, arrives at a photo opportunity on March 30, 1999, via dog sled. Dog sledding has been a method of transportation in the Arctic for indigenous peoples for over 2,000 years. Many sled dogs are also trained to find their way home in the middle of a blizzard, bark when dangerous animals are near, track caribou, and locate seal holes for hunters.

An Inuit in a traditional umiak skin boat watches bowhead whales during a whale hunt.

By Sea

For getting around on the water, there were two options: kayaks and umiaks. Built to carry one to three people, kayaks were stitched together using sealskins or caribou hides that were then stretched over a frame of wood or antlers. Waterproof and extremely lightweight, kayaks could be carried over land for extremely long distances.

The Inuit often spoke of "wearing" their kayaks. This is because in the water, a paddler would button the bottom of his skin parka to the edge of the kayak's cockpit. The result was so snug that no water could get in and the paddler could never fall out—not even if the kayak flipped over.

While kayaks were used for hunting seals, umiaks were necessary for going after larger animals such as walruses and whales. Traditionally, they were also used to transport a large group of people who were moving to an island. Up to twenty people could sit in the open umiaks, which were also made of sealskin or walrus hide stretched over wood or whalebone frames.

CHANGING TIMES

Today, few Arctic groups continue to live completely traditional lifestyles. Instead, most residents mix traditional and contemporary ways of life. For instance, an Inuit family may live in a wooden house with electricity and plumbing, but sleep in skin tents or igloos when out

The village of Umanaq in Greenland is a typical Arctic town. Residents make their money from fishing and tourism, and have adapted to the harsh climate.

hunting. Kids may eat pizza, but for a treat, they may dig into a plate of muktuk.

Although the Arctic is slowly becoming less remote and isolated than it once was, this extreme environment, with its climate and geography, plant and animal life, and rich human traditions, is still unique. And while scientists talk about it thawing out a little every year because of global warming, it is certain that the icy Arctic won't be melting away anytime soon.

GLOSSARY

Arctic Circle An imaginary ring around the northern portion of the globe that marks the beginning of the Arctic region at a latitude of 66.5 degrees north of the equator.

aurora borealis Giant explosions of charged sun particles that come hurtling toward Earth's magnetic poles and light up the northern skies with colorful shimmers. Also called northern lights.

biome A geographic region with its own specific plant and animal life.

blubber Thick layer of fat that covers the body of an animal like a blanket.

bog Wet, spongy ground.

carrion Decaying flesh of a dead body that becomes food for animals.

conifers Plants or trees, such as pines, that remain green all year.

dehydrate To lose water or body fluids.

dormant Sluggish, asleep, inactive.

global warming The gradual heating up of Earth due to the release of harmful pollutants into the atmosphere.

Greenland The world's largest island, 85 percent of which is covered with ice.

hypothermia Dangerous decrease in body temperature.

ice age A time in which world temperatures decreased and glaciers spread across Earth.

Inuit Native group that lives in the Arctic regions of Canada, Alaska, and Greenland.

larkspur A tall Arctic plant that flowers.

latitude Invisible lines on maps and globes that measure the horizontal distance north and south of Earth's equator.

lichen Plantlike vegetation that is a mixture of fungus and algae and can grow basically anywhere.

lousewort A red Arctic wildflower.

mammoth Prehistoric hairy elephant.

monkshood A tall Arctic plant.

North Pole The (very cold) northernmost tip of Earth.

omnivore One who eats animals and vegetation.

oxytrope A purple Arctic wildflower.

permafrost A layer of permanently frozen earth that lies beneath Arctic topsoil.

pigment A coloring matter in plant and animal cells and tissues.

pingo A cone-shaped hill with a core of pure ice.

scavenger Animal that feeds on others' leftovers.

scurvy A disease caused by lack of vitamin C, which causes bleeding and loss of teeth.

sinew A tendon that can be used as thread or cord.

taiga Russian word for wet subarctic forest of conifers (spruce and firs).

tundra Russian word for a marshy area without trees.

FOR MORE INFORMATION

Alaska Native Heritage Center
8800 Heritage Center Drive
Anchorage, AK 99506
(907) 330-8000
Web site: http://www.alaskanative.net

Anchorage Museum of History and Art
121 West Seventh Avenue
Anchorage, AK 99501
(907) 343-4326
Web site: http://www.anchoragemuseum.org

Arctic Institute of North America
The University of Calgary
2500 University Drive NW
Calgary, AB, T2N 1N4
Canada
(403) 220-7515
Web site: http://www.ucalgary.ca/aina

Arctic Studies Center
Department of Anthropology
National Museum of Natural History
Smithsonian Institution
Washington, DC 20560-0112
(202) 357-2682
Web site http://www.mnh.si.edu/arctic

International Arctic Research Center
930 Koyukuk Drive
P.O. Box 757340
Fairbanks, AK 99775-7340
(907) 474-7413
Web site http://www.iarc.uaf.edu

U.S. Fish and Wildlife Service
Arctic National Wildlife Refuge
101 Twelfth Avenue, Room 236, Box 20
Fairbanks, AK 99701
Web site http://www.r7.fws.gov/nwr/arctic/arctic.html

Web Sites

Due to the changing nature of Internet links, the Rosen
Publishing Group, Inc., has developed an online list of Web
sites related to the subject of this book. This site is updated
regularly. Please use this link to access the list:

http://www.rosenlinks.com/lee/arct

FOR FURTHER READING

Brimner, Larry Dane. *Polar Mammals*. New York: Children's Press, 1997.

Crisler, Lois. *Arctic Wild: The Remarkable True Story of One Couple's Adventure Among Wolves*. Guilford, CT: The Lyons Press, 1996.

Ehrlich, Gretel. *This Cold Heaven: Seven Seasons in Greenland*. New York: Pantheon Books, 2001.

Flowers, Pam, and Ann Dixon. *Alone Across the Arctic: One Woman's Epic Journey by Dog Team*. Portland, OR: Alaska Northwest Books, 2001.

Lopez, Barry Holstun. *Arctic Dreams: Imagination and Desire in a Northern Landscape*. New York: Vintage Books, 2001.

Sirling, Ian. *Polar Bears*. Ann Arbor, MI: University of Michigan Press, 1998.

Steger, Will. *Over the Top of the World: Explorer Will Steger's Trek Across the Arctic*. New York: Scholastic Press, 1997.

Waterman, Jonathan. *Arctic Crossing: A Journey Through the Northwest Passage and Inuit Culture*. New York: Knopf, 2001.

BIBLIOGRAPHY

Allaby, Michael. *Biomes of the World—Volume 1: The Polar Regions*. Danbury, CT: Grolier Educational, 1999.

Lynch, Wayne. *A is for Arctic: Natural Wonders of a Polar World*. Willowdale, ON: Firefly Books, 1996.

Sayle, April Pulley. *Tundra*. New York: Henry Holt and Company, 1994.

Younkin, Paula. *Indians of the Arctic and Subarctic* (First Americans Series). New York: Facts on File, 1992.

INDEX

About the Author

Sheldon Brooks is a freelance writer.

Photo Credits

Cover © John Conrad/Corbis; pp. 1, 3, 39 Earth Scenes © Johnny Johnson; pp. 4–5 © Bryan and Cherry Alexander Photography; p. 7 © Geoatlas 2003; p. 8 Animals Animals © D. Cox/OSF; pp. 10–11 Earth Scenes © Eastcott/Momatiuk; p. 14 Earth Scenes © Donna Ikenberry; p. 16 Earth Scenes © Joe McDonald; pp. 19, 32–33 Animals Animals © Erwin and Peggy Bauer; pp. 22–23 Animals Animals © D. Allan/OSF; p. 24 Animals Animals © Terry G. Murphy; p. 26 Animals Animals © Rosing, N./OSF ; p. 27 Animals Animals © Joe McDonald; p. 29 Animals Animals © Karni Morris; p. 30 Animals Animals © Norbert Rosing; p. 35 Animals Animals © Richard Kolar; p. 36 Animals Animals © Dominique Braud; p. 37 Animals Animals © Stouffer Prod.; p. 38 © Animals Animals; pp. 40–41 © Fred Bruemmer/Peter Arnold, Inc.; pp. 42, 52 © Michael Sewell/Peter Arnold, Inc.; p. 44 Animals Animals © Eastcott/Momatiuk; p. 46 © Galen Rowell/Corbis; p. 47 © Chlaus Lotscher/Peter Arnold, Inc.; p. 50 © AFP/Corbis; p. 53 Earth Scenes © Bradley W. Stahl.

Designer: Thomas Forget; Editor: Annie Sommers;
Photo Researcher: Adriana Skura